MIRACLE STAGES

by

MARY JO KRAUS

Preface and Epilogue

by

DIANE VENEGONI

A PRODUCTION OF MARY JO'S CLOSET

ISBN: 979-8-218-66493-0

Correspondence may be sent to:

dijobook@gmail.com

DEDICATION

The world is full of heroes and heroines but when they are your people, it is very, very special.

This book is dedicated to all those featured as Heroes and Heroines at the end of this story because they are all what allowed me to survive and celebrate this miracle.

In one way or another, they all kept me going through their faith, encouragement and love.

Heroes and Heroines, I salute you!

Miracle Stages

PREFACE

LAYING THE PREMISE

BY DIANE THE PATIENT

It was the day before New Year's Eve and my friend Mary Jo and I were looking forward to a New Year's Eve party.

It was the first party we had been invited to for a few years. We both enjoy being with family and friends at the stroke of midnight. Mary Jo was making desserts, and it took her almost all day because she was making everything from scratch.

I was not feeling well so I was in my usual spot on the couch, watching TV. I started feeling worse that day and also into the next day. My legs were aching, and I had a terrible headache. It was getting worse, so I called my doctor and he informed me that it was probably the flu, so he gave me the regular treatment of drinking plenty of fluids, rest and take Tylenol. We decided not to go to the party because I didn't want to give anyone else my flu and really, I wasn't physically up to going.

1

New Year's Day, I was feeling a little better, but we stayed home, watched movies, and just hung out because we had a big week ahead of us. I still had my headache when I went to bed that night, but I was able to sleep. In the middle of the night, I woke up with a throbbing headache, sick to my stomach and started throwing up. I woke Mary Jo and she put a cold rag on my head like she always does when I am sick. I went back to bed with chills and sweating but was able to fall back to sleep.

I don't remember anything from the time I fell back to sleep till seven days later.

CHAPTER 01

THE BEGINNING OF THE JOURNEY

And sleep she did. She was gone for what seemed like a century. Stages in our emotions are so changing and frightening that it is a small wonder we can survive them. While my friend was in a state that she did not remember I was going through more emotions than I thought possible.

I figured we could celebrate next New Year's Eve but now there was the realization that there would not BE another New Year's Eve with my friend.

It all began a couple of days before the new year. Di was not feeling good and as usual I was the worrying mother. She said her head was hurting bad and her legs were aching a lot. Her temperature was a couple of degrees high but we both assumed it was a virus. I rubbed her head a lot at her request which led me to believe it really hurt bad.

On the second day we thought we should call the

doctor and did so. He said there was a virus going around and so we followed up with aspirin and bed rest.

New Year's Eve was going to be a big deal this year. My nephew Mike and his wife Maur were having a party. As a family, we usually did not see everyone on this holiday, so this year was special. I was busy making a special cake for this occasion and was busy in the kitchen. As the day progressed, Di said there was no way she could go so I called and cancelled but said I would drop the cake off for someone else to take.

I was really disappointed but there was no way I would leave Diane while she was sick. Most people would leave their friend and go to the party, after all, it was just the flu, but that was not what our friendship was about. We were there for each other no matter how small or large the difficulty.

CHAPTER 02

WHAT MADE IT SO SPECIAL

This wasn't an ordinary friendship. We had met in high school, so it had been 45 years of being together every chance we got.

Neither one of us had married, so soulmates was the word, I guess. We never tired of each other, always enjoying every minute together and very protective of each other.

I was a senior in high school, and she was a sophomore when we met. I think we took to each other so quickly because I was a little older and she looked up to me. I am a pretty insecure person so that was a real plus in a friendship. She made me feel like I was somebody. Always being overweight had given me more than a bad opinion of myself. I had so much to give and no one special to give it to. Here was my chance to be somebody special.

She was a person who was a follower, and I was a

leader, if I knew where I was going. The first summer of 1964 I spent so much time at her house. Diane's mom was a lot like me, and we became very close right from the start. Her family made me feel like I was really great. Not to say I didn't love my family very much, but I always felt I was less than them.

My mom and I never got along, and, in my heart, I felt she didn't respect or love me like my two sisters. This was my hang-up; my mom did her best but nevertheless that was how I felt.

I spent every moment at Diane's house because it made me feel good. It is hard to explain, when you think so little of yourself, how attached you can become to something that makes you feel like you belong. So began a lasting friendship that flourished into a relationship that was, I guess, hard for other people to understand.

At my house, I had my little sister, who I adored but I took care of her so there was no one to try and understand my depression or silly feelings. I was alone at home. My mom and I were not close. I felt very inferior to her and although I was a daddy's girl, he only loved me if it was ok with mom.

My older sister Barb was married and we had become somewhat closer because of her children, who, besides Diane and my younger sister Sue, were my life. There were three at that time - Mark, Kathy, and Mike.

One of the stipulations of being my friend was to love my sisters, and my nieces and nephews. The first summer I met Diane was 1964, the year I graduated from high school. I had a group of good friends at high school, but again, they were thin and dating and I never felt I had a grasp on how they felt.

I needed to be first in someone's life. I catered to my high school friends, gave them parties, showers, sang for their weddings, sent them birthday cards and then they just forgot me. Just forgot me.

Little by little my life was Diane. The years went by and then she graduated from high school and then the years of work began. Little would I know, that the first day of my retirement would be the worst day of my life.

Miracle Stages

CHAPTER 03

THE BEGINNING OF WHAT I THOUGHT WOULD BE THE END

I delivered the cake, and everyone had a wonderful time at the New Year's Eve party. My cake, which now I wondered if all the bad that was going to happen went into that cake, was the worst cake I ever made for no apparent reason. All the ingredients were good, but the cake was tasteless.

News Year's Day came and went, and Di felt a little better. Bedtime came and I went to bed to be woken up by Di, sick to her stomach. I held her head as I always did but she seemed to be really not feeling good. I figured her stomach was sick because of her bad headache. I helped her back to bed and went back to my room thinking she would sleep the rest of the night.

A couple of hours later, I heard her in the bathroom again, but she did not call me, so I thought she was OK. She went back to bed, and I went back to sleep. That could have been the last time I talked to her.

I was to get up extra early the next day to drive some friends to the airport for a very early flight. It was to be a long drive, there and back, and then to their house because I was to watch their dogs.

If Diane had come to my room even two hours later, I would have been gone, she would have been home alone and would have died with no medical attention.

Instead, I was awakened suddenly by a voice I did not recognize in distress, I jumped out of bed and tried to talk to her.

It was 6:15 on January 2, 2009. There was nothing she was saying that was familiar and my heart began to pound as I called 911.

The only thing that she seemed sure about was that she kept saying her teeth were falling out. I thought she had a stroke and I felt terrified as I had been with my dad when this happened to him.

I could hardly hold the phone and my mouth was so dry, my speech was impaired as I called my sisters. The walk down my hall seemed to have no floor as my feet and legs seemed not to hold me up.

I called my younger sister and said something is wrong with Diane, I think she had a stroke. The words seemed to stick in my throat, and I could not believe what I was saying. She said I will be right there.

I tried again to talk to Diane, thinking this was a bad dream and I would surely wake up. Again, her answers did not coincide with my questions as I dialed the phone to call my older sister Barb. For some reason no one answered, and I left a message. The message was returned almost immediately and with a calming voice, my sister said she would meet me at the hospital.

I hung up and somehow walked Diane into the living room where she collapsed on the couch. Now she did not know where she lived. Her skin was white and clammy, and I thought I could never live through the future.

When the paramedics came, I told them what had happened, but they were no help for my emotions. Fear took over my mind and all I could think of was getting help. I asked if they thought she had had a stroke, but they would not comment at all. They proceeded to pick her up by her hands and legs and I stopped them. She was not comfortable. I wanted a stretcher and a blanket.

My younger sister arrived right after the paramedics. She was pale and trying to pretend everything would be OK but I was not believing anything right now. She told me to go with the ambulance and she would take care of our dog Augy.

How I remembered to take Diane's wallet so I had her information I will never know. I followed the ambulance to the hospital. The highway was empty, but I would not have seen anyone even if they were there. My eyes were focused only on the road that was to lead me to my soulmate, my life.

CHAPTER 04

ENTERING THE UNKNOWN

I felt cold and trembling as I approached the emergency room. I ran to the entrance and saw my older sister standing at the desk trying to give the information they needed. She hugged me but I felt nothing but terror. They directed me immediately to the room. No one could have kept me at that desk. It would be intolerable not to be at Diane's side.

I ran to the room I was instructed to, where I found her in the bed now making no sense and so distressed that she would not stay in bed. The movements were erratic, and she had to be held down and covered up constantly. Her legs were climbing out of bed, and she was violently trying to go somewhere, almost as if she was trying to get out of her body.

My only thought was to hold her, so she knew in her mind that I was there, even though her brain was somewhere else. My sister thought it might be extreme dehydration, which could cause out of mind reactions. I wanted to believe her, but the possibility was so far from what I was seeing.

The only word she was saying was NO because she did not want to stay in bed. The nurses' said dehydration was possible but from the way they were treating her so quickly, I was as unsure of that diagnosis as I could be.

They took a lot of blood, and we could not leave her side for an instant. If we had not been there to help the nurses hold her down, I don't know how they could have worked on her.

My sisters reminded me, I should call Diane's sister Lee Ann and they said they would do it for me since I was so focused on My Dear Friend.

A cat scan was done immediately which ruled out a stroke. My mind was going so many different ways between worry and the future that my body was functioning on autopilot.

The person lying in that bed was my life, talking to her to calm her looked like it was a fruitless action, but I had to let her know I was there to protect her.

By this time my brother-in-law was there too. My family is such a source of joy to me, they are caregivers and friends to ease a heavy heart. When I could take a minute, I called Lee Ann myself.

She had gotten a hold of Di's sister Donna in Cape Girardeau, and I had to report I really didn't know much but she was in terrible shape. Lee Ann said she would be right there, and she would take care of letting Donna know what we knew so far.

The room was small, but the nurses never asked anyone to leave, partly I think because she would hurt herself with climbing out of bed. We covered her constantly, she had no sense of modesty, coherence, or recognition of any of us.

What seemed like hours passed and Diane's older sister Lee Ann arrived.

I hugged her but again I felt nothing but terror. It was so unlike me not to react to hugs. My nature is surrounded by hugs, I live for them, but I was not living, I was surviving.

My whole self was consumed with the thought of

tragedy.

One of my nieces was there also. We did not have any idea what we were dealing with, but we were instructed to wear a mask in case of something contagious. I told my niece not to go into the room. Another loved one getting sick was something I would never forgive myself for letting happen.

My family was a source of pride to me at that time. My nieces, who I had watched grow up and cared for and loved like my own, were now grown women and taking care of me.

My younger sister Sue kept in contact with her doctor friend, Kevin, who was the husband of her childhood friend, Brenda. If it hadn't been for those two people telling me different information about what the doctors in the hospital were saying was right or wrong, I do not know what I would have done. This was a major help to answer all my questions.

They tried to do a spinal tap in the room, but Di was moving too much. A spinal tap was what Kevin, Sue's doctor friend, said they should do although that sounded a lot more serious than dehydration. A spinal tap was done next because of her extreme headache.

They rolled her down the hall and I could not go. This was unacceptable to me. What if she needed me, what if she called for me? Just as she went away, my youngest niece arrived; she melted into my arms and sobbed.

This was not like her; she hated to cry in front of people. I tried to console her by saying Diane will be fine. No other words would come out. If I did not say that I would have fallen apart.

CHAPTER 05

NOW WE KNOW, NOW WE WAIT

We sat in the waiting room trying to be optimistic but how could it not be something very serious with action so unlike my Diane. Not to know me was inconceivable.

My brother-in-law Bill, who has always been the rock of our family, tried to be calm, but I knew something was very, very wrong. They sent us back to the first room to wait for results and soon the infectious disease doctor came out.

My family and Lee Ann were standing behind me when the doctor said she had pneumococcus meningitis, and he did not know if she would live. My body felt like it collapsed but I was still standing. He was telling me I might lose my soul mate, my future, my life.

Something kicked in and the only way I could survive this was optimism and the statement, "no, she will be all right ". I kept saying that because the alternative was destruction to my soul. My heart was going fast, and panic attacks were ever so present. When I walked, I felt

19

like I couldn't, when I talked, I felt like my voice was so shaky that I couldn't convey my thoughts.

Soon after she was moved to intensive care. A nurse named John was her first nurse. He was kind and knowledgeable and a bit of relief came to know she was in good hands.

When we went back to the room, blankets were placed on the rails of the bed. I asked why, and the question was when the brain swells, seizures might come. At this time, she was still so agitated she never stopped moving.

Hammering on her head and eyes made me think the head pain was unbearable. I couldn't leave her side because I was afraid she would hurt herself by thrashing so violently. Her legs were up and down; her arms were trying to get her brain to function.

This was a reality now and I wondered how I would survive for her and myself. It was up to God and me to pull her through this. My sister's doctor friend Kevin was in Kansas, and he kept us informed of the optimistic side of this nightmare.

She might die, she might die, she might die was

screaming in my head and I had to do something. I never left her side, holding her arms, covering her body, talking to her, and telling her what happened and that it would be all right.

I asked the doctor if there was hope and he said there was always hope, but the look in his eyes told me we were on the short end of the stick.

He was a very impersonal doctor and I needed someone to comfort me and be on my side. I asked him, please don't be so curt, I am very upset, and I need you to be understanding.

From that time on, he was kinder. The nurses said he had no bedside manner, but he was good. Good! I needed great. We needed a miracle. I don't think my own dying could be any more terrifying than this. It was like someone was killing me a little at a time and I was in a race to survive just like her.

We are two people in one, we feel for each other, so I had my feelings and hers to deal with. For a whole day she moved from up and down, side to side, her face was in constant distress.

CHAPTER 06

THE WAITING BEGINS

My older sister, Barb, was a strong woman who worried about things when and if they happen. Complete opposite of me who always worries about what could happen. I knew Barb was worried.

Di was like a sister to her, and I knew she was aching, in pain and was scared to death. She was a kind person behind the tough demeanor, I knew she would be there for anything I needed.

I sometimes think Barb trusted her sisters without reservation. She was tall in body and mind. She was strong-willed and sure of her feelings even though people didn't always agree with her.

She was the rock of our family and took the place of our mom and dad in wisdom and solidarity.

My younger sister, Sue, has always been protected by me. Neither of us married and it was our job to take care of each other. I knew she was scared she would have to take care of me in the dark of this day.

Her most important job was to stay on the phone to her doctor and nurse friend and give me answers and consolation as much as she could. I am an information person. I want to know why, how, and when to most every situation and this was the most important situation I have ever encountered.

John was working on Diane all the time. She was hooked up to heart, breathing, oxygen pulse rate. She had two IV's in. One for nourishment and one for antibiotics, strong antibiotics. Of course she was catheterized, so keeping her covered was a full-time job. My family and her sisters were so good to me as I look back.

At the time, I was sort of numb to emotion in one way and so vulnerable to emotion in another. My whole being was working on being two people fighting for their lives. Through our whole friendship of 45 years, we have been so protective of one another it was almost too involved to explain. Now we were faced with the ultimate loss all at once.

Now we had to wear a mask all the time until we found

the antibiotic that would work, the doctor said 72 hours would tell.

By this time, my two nephews and their wives were there also. Their eyes seem so sad. They are young adults and I think the shock of losing this generation so soon was very, very hard on all of them. I told them, please don't go in. Meningitis can be contagious and to lose another to this disease that no one knew where it came from would be too hard to imagine. They were there to console me, to make calls, to take care of me and my heart was bursting with gratitude.

As I look back, I wonder if I remembered to say as many thank-you's as I should have. I was so engrossed and so bleak that I might not have been as kind as I should have been.

Donna, Diane's twin had now arrived from Cape Girardeau. Diane's sisters were there for the long haul for me and for each other. They never thought of themselves, they thought of me. They were wonderful to me and with me and for me.

Their wonderful mom had passed away, and now, in

the presence of disaster, Diane's two sisters clasped hands and minds and pulled each other out of the dark depths of illness, in this stage of emotion and of life.

The first full night came and as I sat next to the bed trying to keep Diane from hurting herself, I knew that her sisters sleeping out in the waiting room and my sisters at home, who I had told to go home and sleep because I would need them later, could not REALLY help at all.

I was in this alone I would be the one to make decisions, and if she lived, take care of her. The panic attacks were so frequent, I felt I couldn't breathe. I learned one thing though.

The only thing that helped me was to say Our Fathers, and Hail Marys to escape the fear that was taking over. God helped me. It seems he gives us many different stages for our souls to live out before he calls us home.

He IS there. I prayed for stillness and a comfort for her. I felt like I was going to die with her, but no, I couldn't, I had a job to do, and I had to do it perfectly.

CHAPTER 07

SOMETIMES
GETTING WHAT YOU ASK FOR IS SCARY

And then the silence came she laid her head against one side of the bed and went into a deep sleep. For a while, we were a little relieved, but she was not moving; it was silent.

The doctor said there was no improvement the next day, but it was no worse. The antibiotic was the right one but no guarantee it would work.

If it did work, there was an 80% chance there would be brain damage from the swelling like deafness, retardation, or paralysis. All things that would change our lives completely.

Would I have to walk around with her holding my hand? How would I care for her since my back was weak? My emotions had gone from what was wrong to Oh my God how will we survive this. Together was all I could think.

Throughout our friendship, we have lived our lives around what the other one wanted to do. Giving to each other was the ultimate goal of our friendship. One of the most precious things was the knowing that, no matter what, we would be there for one another, always and forever.

All my energy went to doing all I could to talk to her and let her know I was here. She had to know somewhere in her brain that I was taking care of things and making everything alright.

I asked for stillness for her and what I got was the scariest stillness I hope I ever encounter. Nurses and doctors were going in and out. Each time I would ask what they were doing and how it would affect her. Each time we left the room we had to cleanse our hands and redo our mask.

The only time I left the room was to go to the bathroom or eat. There was a very clear sign that I was in distress. I did not want to eat. I had to eat a little to keep my strength up, but it was a chore. As we would leave the room to eat, only if a nurse was with her, I wondered how anyone would be thinking of food.

The halls were colder than usual; they were silent and

cold, like death. I would walk down the hall and not remember how I got there. I would talk to someone and forget what I had said.

My family were keeping in constant touch. I remember telling my one niece that I felt like I was dying. I don't think she understood that Di and my relationship is one-of-a-kind, how could she.

The nurses would try to explain what they thought had happened. It was too bizarre to imagine. A meningitis germ had gone through her sinuses and got to her brain. The brain was infected and swelling.

After two days she still was not responding to voices, movement or touch. She was in a deep, deep sleep and the neurologist said it was up to the brain to do the work. Her brain had swollen and we were waiting for it to cure itself.

I had always been the one to take care of scary things, how could I let her down and not make this all right? It was two whole days now and the doctors said 72 hours would tell.

The stats were not worse, maybe a little better. A

glimmer of hope took over that could have lifted a mountain. I was grasping at anything. No seizures had occurred. I never took my eyes off the monitor or her.

They talked about septic poison getting into her bloodstream and that would be even worse. She was not responding, and the monitor was fixed to my eyes like it was attached to me.

When the brain doctor came in, he would press really hard on her chest bone. It broke my heart. He was hurting her but that told him she was not in a coma because her face looked in pain. She couldn't eat, naturally, and her thyroid medicine did not come in IV form, so a stomach tube had to be put in through her nose if she didn't wake up soon.

I had no appetite at all, which told me my body too was in distress. I ate only to keep strength up because I was living for two.

Although I felt very, very alone the support from my sisters, Diane's sisters, and my family was incredible. They were there for every step of bad and never thought not to do whatever they could. I knew I was lucky, but this proved I was blessed with people that loved both of us very, very much.

The third day came, and she lay so silent, I yearned to hear her voice. Her sister decided to stay an extra day in the hopes she would wake up.

Late that afternoon her eyes opened. We jumped up and talked to her. When she looked at me and I looked into her eyes there was nothing there. There was no recognition, no emotion, and no sound. I died inside. I figured brain damage had taken her away from me forever. I am a pessimist.

Even though I got through this trying to talk my way out of the fact she might die, I, in my heart, think the worst. She wasn't there. I was Mary Jo and she didn't respond to me; the aching in my soul was so strong, I thought I would never be able to talk to her again. For the first time, I collapsed in the arms of my baby sister and sobbed. She kept saying, whatever this brings we will deal with it, but it wasn't we. This was a personal trial that no one could help me with no matter how hard they tried.

CHAPTER 08

A GLIMMER OF HOPE

Since she at least had her eyes open, the doctors thought that was a good sign for living but we had no idea what kind of living. Would she know who she was or who I was?

Fear swept over me like lava from a volcano. I could feel my body getting hot and sweaty and I couldn't run.

Her IVs were hard to get in and even the smallest thing they did to her, I would hold her hand and talk to her when they were working on her.

Her sisters and I thought we would go get coffee. As I started to leave the room, a startled voice cried out that all three of us heard "Mary Jo."

I stopped and went back to her, told her I would be right back, and a glimmer of hope said her brain knew I was there, it just couldn't let us know.

Later that day the tube had to be put in. Even the nurse hated to do this procedure, but she had to get nourishment. My sister said I should not put myself through watching the tube go in, but I knew I had to be there talking to her telling her it would be over in a minute and it would be alright. The look of fear and pain on her face will never leave my mind.

I felt I had betrayed her by letting pain come to her. I told her I was so sorry, but she had to have nourishment. As I looked into her anguished face, I felt this was the rest of our lives. This is how it would be. Talking to a shell that didn't understand and couldn't respond. Grief, fear, sadness came over me, our time together was over. A little bit of me died then.

Now there was the problem of preventing her from pulling out the tube that was in her nose. I did not want it to be put back in, so it was my job to make sure it did not come out. Just that simple.

No one else seemed to be so attentive to this fact, but I was obsessed with it. No one was going to have to do that tube again. Not on my watch. To help prevent the tube from being pulled out, the nurse put these big mittens that looked like boxing gloves on so she couldn't grasp the feeding tube. This worked for a while and then Diane became so agitated with them that I thought it was cruel to have them on.

So, back to the bedside vigilance. If I could prevent any suffering from her, that was how it was going to be. When I wasn't there or someone I could trust wasn't there, we would put the glove on her left hand. She is right-handed, why the left?

A new scare. She was not moving her right arm. At first, I thought maybe it was just tired. She had thrust around so much in bed her body had to be sore, but then it continued, the right arm was just lying there. I mentioned it, and, yes, other people noticed it too.

This was the 4th day. Her eyes didn't have such a faraway look to them. There was no response, no speech, but her eyes looked more focused. This was good. Maybe she was starting to think.

My brain said hurrah, but my heart was still so sad and scared. I did not want to get my hopes up, because I really don't think I could take a letdown. The stats were looking better, she was getting nourishment, and the doctors were optimistic.

We were on our way. My God could this be true! She just may come out of this alive. But happiness was so drenched with worry. How would she come out. Could I take care of her? How would this new person be; deaf, paralyzed, handicapped, mentally challenged? My soul felt like we had cleared the destruction but what about all the dust?

She would not want to be a burden, although I would do anything to keep her as long as she **WAS HAPPY!** That was the key - as long as **SHE** was happy.

CHAPTER 09

ON OUR WAY

The morning of the 5th day, Diane's other sister went home from staying the night and before she left, we were able to see a little calmness and happiness in Diane's face.

She had made friends with her hand mitten. She looked at it as if it was the first friend she ever saw. She was smiling at me now, which made my heart sing - but - she was smiling the same at everyone now. This meant no recognition of certain people.

But she was happy, that was the main thing. I laughed a little that morning because I could see her smile. After her sister left, my sister stayed with her so I could go home and shower and sort some things out.

When I returned, I met my niece as I got off the elevator. She said my friend said "Hi" to her. I rushed to the room. My heart was pounding, my legs were weak. Maybe I could hear her voice, maybe she would know me.

As I walked into the room my sister said she said Hi to my nephew also. I walked over to the other side of the bed; my hands were trembling. I was selfish, I wanted her to say my name and recognize me.

She was looking the other way and I said "Di," and she turned her head and said "What?"

What turned into the sweetest word I ever heard, it was her voice, her response, and I wanted to scream in rejoicing song.

She was better, she was here, she was responding. And then I asked the scariest question I will probably ever ask. "Diane, what's my name?" and she said "Mary Jo."

The relief was immeasurable; happiness was not enough to explain the relief that she was a person, not a vegetable. My heart was so full of gratitude. Could we have conquered our journey of terror? I think so and my whole body felt like a warm explosion came from my feet up to my brain out to my smile.

That day, the 5th day, progressed in leaps and bounds. It seemed like every hour she knew something else. She still had her friend on her hand. My sister named him

Wilson. That was **OK** though.

She had died inside, and it was like she was born again, and everything was balloons and roses. The nurses were prettier to her, and she smiled all the time. Her right hand was still not moving right but we could deal with that. It worried me a lot, but she was happy ----She did not know or care that her hand was not working, and she insisted she could get up.

Everything she had been through really did not happen in her mind and it was hard to get her to understand she couldn't do certain things.

On the 6th day the tube came out because she could swallow **OK**, and it was an easy procedure for her. Then it was time to eat, to feed herself. She couldn't use a fork or judge her mouth. A sickening feeling came over me. It was that nasty reality again that things would never be the same.

As she progressed, she wasn't as happy. Not sad. She was just coming back to reality. She was very weak and could not walk.

Therapy was inevitable but she was on the mend, the

stats looked good, and I was beginning to go into the stage of fear she would not fully recover.

It is funny, what we expect. When the worst is over, we automatically want more and more of what is comfortable.

The 6th day they got her up and she had no strength whatsoever, but she still thought she did. Now it was time to be moved to another room, out of intensive care, and again I started to worry if I could stay with her. Some people would not think this is a big thing, but I did and I had to deal with it because no one would understand.

We moved out of intensive care and into a room where the nurses not only said it was alright to stay in the room but got me a bed.

They started to talk about where she would go for therapy and the sickening feeling came back because a nursing facility was mentioned. I have always had a phobia about nursing homes and the thought of it made me sick inside.

I wouldn't be able to stay and that upset me. It reminded me that we were not young anymore and this was coming too soon. With the grace of God, and I do believe he had a hand in it, we were able to go to the hospital rehab.

To my delight, I could stay, it was not like a nursing home, and it was wonderful. My appetite was coming back which told me my brain is telling me it is OK, and we will be going home soon, very soon.

I began to eat some of the wonderful snacks that my niece, Kathy, had sent up for us. Until now I couldn't indulge in this wonderful gift.

Within two days she was walking, feeding herself, dressing herself, and we were in heaven. Therapy was going quickly, and I started to relax a little and know it was almost over.

CHAPTER 10

A LITTLE BIT OF HEAVEN

Two weeks to the day, we walked out of that hospital together. Two was again. It was smooth sailing from here on out.

Stages of emotions can cause miracles. God gives us stages of sorrow, anticipation, terror, happiness, love, acceptance, and any other feeling we need to be able to understand other's needs. I know miracle stages exist because I had one!

As the time passes, there are many nights that panic attacks come into my room at night, reliving that horrible night.

A year has passed now and the fear of when tragedy will strike again is ever present. The stages that saw me and Diane through those dark hours will be ever present in our brains. Life is so unpredictable.

It is truly one stage after another, getting to the other side of the mountains that we must climb because that is the reality of life. The climbing makes the coasting more enjoyable and appreciated.

I guess it makes us stronger, wiser, and more adapted to the trials of life but, nonetheless just as scary, just as lonely and just as uncontrollable as God would have them. He is the only thing we are sure of in our solitary stages of life.

EPILOGUE

BY DIANE THE PATIENT

A chance of me not coming through this got around like wildfire. I was put on everyone's prayer list at their churches. Catholic, Lutheran, Baptist and even those who did not attend church kept me in their prayers and in their hearts, not only for me but for Mary Jo and our families.

The infectious disease doctor found the right antibiotic that took effect right away. I was so very fortunate!!!

Everyone knew the chain of prayers which were circulating was being answered. I was in intensive care for seven days, a regular room and rehab for a few days.

I went to rehab to strengthen my endurance and stability. I had to bathe, get dressed, make my bed and be able to do normal things in the kitchen.

I told them the kitchen thing was not necessary because I was rarely in that room. The main thing I had to accomplish was being able to walk up a flight of steps.

We lived on the 2nd floor, and I had to do this myself. I did not want to put Mary Jo through any more pain or heartache.

I was progressing so fast I was called the miracle child; I was sixty.

Meningitis, I found out mostly struck young children and young adults and seldom showed up in older adults. The doctors really didn't know what caused this.

I remember my rehab room. I was so fortunate it was like my own little hotel room, very bright and cheery and the physical therapy (PT) people were so nice.

The most important thing was Mary Jo got to stay with me every second to watch me progress and I definitely wanted to make her happy and start healing her painful heart.

Heroes and Heroines

Mary Jo Kraus

Diane Venegoni

Diane and Mary Jo

Mary Jo's Mom and Dad   Dorothy and Walter (Bud)

Sisters: Barb, Mary Jo, Sue

Barb
Family Matriarch

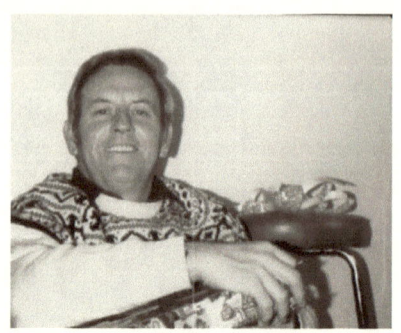

Bill M. Family Rock
and Barb's Husband

Bill and Barb

Sue

John and Pat Diane's Parents

Diane's Sister Lee Ann　　Diane's Twin Sister Donna

Sisters, Lee Ann with Diane

Twins, Donna with Diane

Sue and Barb with Diane

Diane with Barb

Diane With Sue

Diane with Connie, Sue's Best Friend

Diane and Mary Jo

with Nieces and Nephews

Back Row from left

Mike M.

Mark M.

Mark K.

Kathy M. K.

Front Row from left

Nancy

Diane

Mary Jo

Kelly M. M.

NEPHEWS

Mark M. with Wife Nancy

Mike M.

NIECES

Kathy M.K. with Husband Mark

Kelly M.M.

Dr. Kevin G. and Brenda.

Sue's doctor friend, married to Sue's childhood friend.

Diane and Mary Jo with Augy

We have no photos of John, the nurse, or of all the other doctors, nurses, technicians, and hospital staff at **Missouri Baptist Hospital**, in St. Louis, MO. They are also true heroes and heroines in this story.

Their kindness, experience, professionalism, and expertise were essential in all aspects of Diane's recovery, and we thank them from the bottom of our hearts.

Miracle Stages

ACKNOWLEDGMENTS

It is my sincere pleasure to acknowledge, praise and thank the people who made this book happen. With their knowledge, their patience, their interest in my story and all the hours that matured "Miracle Stages" to be a book.

They are Jan Kraus, who is my cousin and a childhood friend. She read my story and said people should be aware of this. Then she went to work and did all her tricks to make it happen.

Thanks to another cousin, Judy Kraus, who also was a big part of my childhood. Her countless hours of typing, reading and helping with any aspect she could to make our jobs easier.

Thank you, Kathleen Kelly, who did our initial edits and Kathy Kon who did the final edits. Thank you, our Beta Readers; Cathy Dickherber Pilant, Kathy Kon and Sue Kraus.

Miracle Stages

ABOUT THE AUTHORS

Mary Jo Kraus

Born in St. Louis in the mid-forties, I was raised in a loving, strict family of parents and two sisters. I worked in the corporate world for 34 years and then in special education. I love family, crafts, travel and enjoying my retired life with my soulmate.

Diane Venegoni

I lived in St. Louis all my life with a happy childhood with my parents, a twin sister and an older sister. After high school, I worked 60 years at various jobs. I like to work, gamble, be with family and hangout with my better half.